Getting Started in Dried Flower Craft

BARBARA H. AMLICK

The Bruce Publishing Company / New York
Collier-Macmillan Limited / London

Copyright © 1971 The Bruce Publishing Company

All rights reserved. No part of this book may be reproduced or transmitted in any form or by any means, electronic or mechanical, including photocopying, recording or by any information storage and retrieval system, without permission in writing from the Publisher.

Library of Congress Catalog Card Number: 70-152291

THE BRUCE PUBLISHING COMPANY
866 THIRD AVENUE, NEW YORK, NEW YORK 10022

COLLIER-MACMILLAN CANADA, LTD., TORONTO, ONTARIO

Made in the United States of America

Getting Started in Dried Flower Craft

Books in the *Getting Started* series

African Crafts

Batik

Ceramics

Dried Flower Craft

Macramé

Handmade Rugs

Prints and Patterns

Leathercraft

Candlemaking

Egg Decoration

Papercraft

Kitemaking

CONTENTS

INTRODUCTION   vii

1 DRYING PLANT MATERIAL   1
    Tools and Supplies
    Drying Methods
    Storing Dried Material

2 GATHERING PLANT MATERIAL   13
    Selecting Plant Material for Drying

3 DRIED PLANT ARRANGEMENTS   31
    Types of Arrangements
    Containers and Holders
    Selecting Material for an Arrangement
    Making a Dried Arrangement
    Caring for an Arrangement

4 PRESSED-FLOWER PICTURES 51
    Tools and Supplies
    Selecting Material for Pictures
    Pressing Plant Material
    Assembling a Pressed Flower Picture

BIBLIOGRAPHY 67

INDEX 69

INTRODUCTION

Drying flowers is a hobby which can be enjoyed by anyone who loves flowers. No special skills are required to dry flowers successfully or to use them in making dried arrangements and designs. The few tools and supplies which are needed for this craft are easily available and inexpensive. If you do not have a "green thumb" or own a garden, the fields and roadsides will furnish a wealth of weeds and wildflowers. When dried, these can be as attractive as their cultivated cousins. Many florists' flowers are also good for drying, and for the city or apartment dweller this is an excellent way to stretch a small flower budget.

Drying plants in order to preserve them is an ancient craft. In prehistoric times, people learned to dry various grasses, roots, seeds, and fruits for food. By the Middle Ages, plants were also being dried for their medicinal properties and for use as beverages, seasonings, spices, perfumes, and insecticides. The colonial housewife was probably the first to dry flowers for decorative purposes and to use them in arrangements and winter bouquets. If you visit Mount Vernon, Monticello, or the Williamsburg restoration, you will see many examples of these early dried arrangements. Drying and pressing flowers continued to be popular pastimes in the Victorian era. Some of the elaborate arrangements of this period, preserved under bell glasses, have survived to this day and can be seen in the collections of various museums.

About fifteen years ago, there was a revival of interest in drying flowers for decorative purposes, and the craft has been increasing in scope and popularity ever since. It is now possible, with the aid of several new products and processes, to create dried arrangements and designs that not only last a long time but also preserve the original beauty and colors of the natural materials.

Getting Started in Dried Flower Craft

1 DRYING PLANT MATERIAL

Dried flowers are those which have been naturally or artificially dehydrated for use in artistically arranged displays. The drying procedures preserve the usually ephemeral beauty of flowers and plant material, although not all flowers lend themselves well to the drying processes. Those that do, however, can last a long time, bringing much enjoyment and satisfaction to plant lovers.

You might think that the first step in drying flowers would be to gather all the plant material that you want to preserve. It is best, however, to collect all the necessary equipment first and then review all the drying processes. In this way you can choose the method most suitable for the type of plants you will be working with, and you will have the appropriate equipment at hand.

TOOLS AND SUPPLIES

Before you start gathering flowers and other plant material for drying, have the following equipment on hand:

Scissors or flower shears

String

Masking or freezer tape

Floral tape (brown and green)

Florist's wire (No. 18 or No. 21; No. 30)

Wire cutters

Hammer

Small camel's hair brush

Household cement (Uncle Elmer's Glue-all or Sobo)

Clear plastic spray (Krylon or regular-type hair spray)

Glycerin

Silica gel

Tin boxes or coffee cans (with covers)

Wide-mouthed glass jars (with covers)

You may already have some of these supplies in the house; the others are available at a local florist, hardware store, or five-and-ten.

The glycerin, which is sold in all drugstores, is used for preserving foliage. Buy it in bulk; it is less expensive that way.

Silica gel is a dry chemical compound. For many years it has been widely used in industry because of its ability to absorb large amounts of water vapor. More recently it has found popular acceptance as a drying medium for flowers. It is especially packaged for this purpose under the trade name Flower Dri, and is readily available at most florists. Although silica gel is quite expensive, it fortunately does not deteriorate and can be used and reused indefinitely. A four-pound can should be sufficient to start with.

DRYING METHODS

Most plant material can be preserved for a considerable period of time simply by removing its natural moisture. This can be accomplished in several ways: by air drying, by pressing, or by using a dehydrating medium such as silica gel.

The choice of drying method is largely dependent on the type of plant material that is to be processed. Air drying, for example, is excellent for seedpods, grasses, and berries. It is also the best method for drying flowers such as goldenrod or yarrow, which are composed of many small florets. Large-petaled flowers, such as roses and zinnias, tend to shrivel and lose color when air dried. Better results are obtained with these if they are placed in a dehydrating medium.

Pressing has limited use in processing material for arrangements; it is extremely useful, though, in drying flowers and foliage for pictures. The pressing method is explained more fully in Chapter 4.

Air Drying

Air drying is by far the easiest of the drying methods. The material to be processed need only be gathered, tied in bunches, and then suspended upside down in a dry place where it is not exposed to the direct rays of the sun. (A word of caution: be sure to tie each bunch tightly with string before hanging it up. Plant stems shrink as they dry, and unless bunches are securely tied, the material may fall out of them.) An attic usually makes an excellent drying area; so does a reasonably dry cellar or garage. If these or similar areas are not available, a closet will serve just as well.

String a length or several lengths of clothesline across the drying area to support the bunches of plants being dried. If you are using a closet, simply tie the plant material to coat hangers and hang these on the clothes rod. Space the bunches far enough apart to allow the air to circulate freely between them. Average plant material can be air dried in two to three weeks; coarse, woody or extremely juicy plants may take somewhat longer. When the process is completed, the plants will feel crisp and dry to the touch.

Silica Gel

There are a number of so-called "dehydrating mediums" which can be used for drying plant material. Of these, the most common are sand, borax, cornmeal, and silica gel.

From my own experience, I find that silica gel gives excellent results, and it is recommended here for several reasons. First

Plant material hung on a line for air drying.

of all, silica gel requires no preliminary preparation. It need not be mixed, washed, or sifted, and it is ready for use just as it comes from the can. Secondly, silica gel leaves no dusty residue on the plants which have been processed in it. Any small grains left clinging to leaves or petals are easily removed with a brush.

Once "wet," silica gel is more readily dried than other dehydrating mediums. It should be noted here that even when silica gel has absorbed its maximum capacity of water vapor, it still looks and feels dry. For this reason a number of pale blue crystals are mixed in with the white grains of the medium. These serve as "indicators"; when their color can no longer be seen, it is time for the medium to be dried.

To dry the "wet" silica gel, spread the gel in a shallow pan and then place the pan in a warm oven (250°F.) for twenty minutes, or until the blue crystals are again visible.

GETTING STARTED IN DRIED FLOWER CRAFT

Plant material hung on a coat hanger for air drying.

Before processing flowers with silica gel, strip off all foliage and cut the stems to a length of two inches. Short stems can easily be lengthened when the time comes to use the flowers in an arrangement.

Wire large marigolds and carnations as shown in Figure 1. Other flowers can also be wired if necessary (see Figure 2).

Fill a tin cake box or coffee can with enough silica gel to cover the bottom to a depth of two inches. When processing spikes of larkspur, delphinium, or snapdragon, a long shoebox makes a more suitable container for the medium.

Place the flowers on top of the silica gel, spacing them at intervals so that they do not touch. Multipetaled flowers, such as zinnias, should be inserted face up. Daisies and other flowers that have a single row of petals should be inserted face down. Roses are best inserted at an angle (Figure 3). Place long flower spikes horizontally on top of the medium.

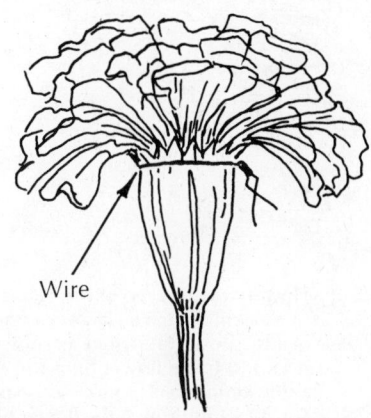

FIGURE 1 Flowers such as marigolds and carnations, which have deep calyxes, should be wired before they are dried. Use No. 30 wire, and twist it very tightly around the calyx. The wire can be snipped off after the flower is dried.

DRYING PLANT MATERIAL

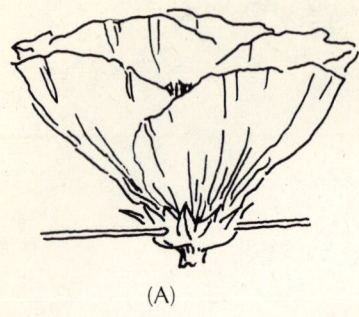
(A)

(B)

(C)

FIGURE 2 Flowers with very short stems, or ones which have large or heavy heads, should be wired as shown in A and B. If the flower does not have a thickened base, push a hook of No. 18 wire through the flower head, as shown in C.

Slowly sprinkle silica gel around each flower. As you work, make certain that it fills any small depressions under or between the petals. When all the flowers are completely covered with the silica gel, place the top on the container and seal it tightly with masking or freezer tape.

Flowers may take anywhere from two to eight days to dry. The exact length of the drying period will, of course, depend on the type of material being processed. After about forty-eight hours, it is a good idea to check the condition of the flowers. Gently brush away a little of the silica gel and test the petals with your finger. If they feel crisp to the touch, processing has been completed. Do not overdry flowers by letting them remain too long in the silica gel; if this happens, they may shatter when handled.

Glycerin

While most foliage can be successfully processed in silica gel, it often becomes brittle and therefore difficult to handle in an arrangement. For this reason certain types of foliage are more frequently processed in glycerin. The glycerin method is essentially a means of preserving foliage; it is not a drying method. Once glycerinated, leaves and branches remain fresh-textured and pliable indefinitely.

Unfortunately, not every type of foliage will absorb glycerin. Elm and mulberry leaves, for example, cannot be preserved by this method. Nor can the glycerin method be used successfully for flowers. Celosia is perhaps the one exception, though this flower too is more often dried than glycerinated.

The glycerin method seems to work better on thick, glossy, or leathery leaves than on thin, delicate ones. Attractive results can be achieved with rhododendron, laurel, privet, bayberry, barberry, crabapple, ivy, periwinkle, and the viburnums. Experiment with various types of foliage; no doubt you will find other excellent subjects to glycerinate.

Processing foliage in glycerin Before processing, wash foliage under cool running water to remove all traces of dust and dirt. Next, fray the bark and inner fibers of the main stem by pounding them with a hammer. If you do not have a hammer handy, a large rock will do the job nicely.

GETTING STARTED IN DRIED FLOWER CRAFT

Foliage stalks which have been frayed with a hammer so that they will absorb the glycerin solution.

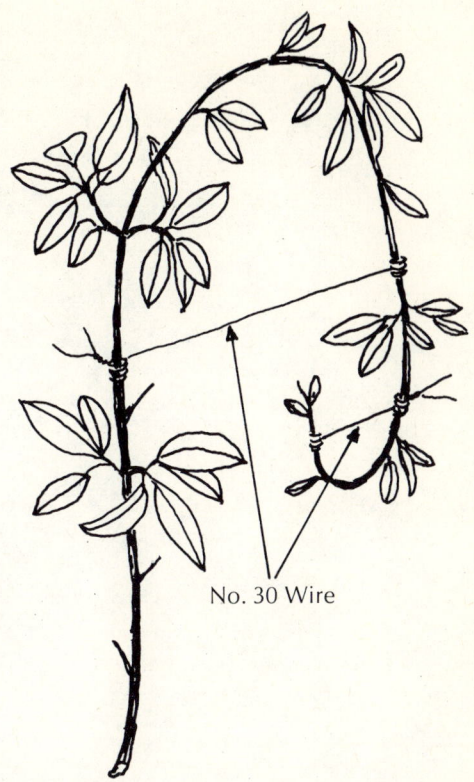

Foliage stalks can be made to curve if wired, as shown. Wire can be removed after processing has been completed.

Now thoroughly mix one part glycerin with two parts water, and pour the mixture into a large jar or a 46-ounce juice can to an approximate depth of four inches.

Stand the foliage in the container for two weeks, or until all the leaves are completely glycerinated. It is a good idea to check the top leaves occasionally for signs of wilting. If this occurs, go over the leaves lightly with a piece of cotton moistened in the glycerin solution. Also check the solution itself to see that it has not all been absorbed; if it has, or if there is less than an inch of the solution remaining, add more to the container. Any leftover solution can be saved, for it is reusable.

Periwinkle and ivy absorb glycerin through their leaves rather than through their stems; so, for processing, they must be fully immersed in the solution. Coil these vines in a shallow bowl, and then add enough solution to cover. If you have trouble keeping the vines submerged, weight them down with a rock.

FIGURE 3   Roses should be inserted in the silica gel at about a 45-degree angle.

DRYING PLANT MATERIAL

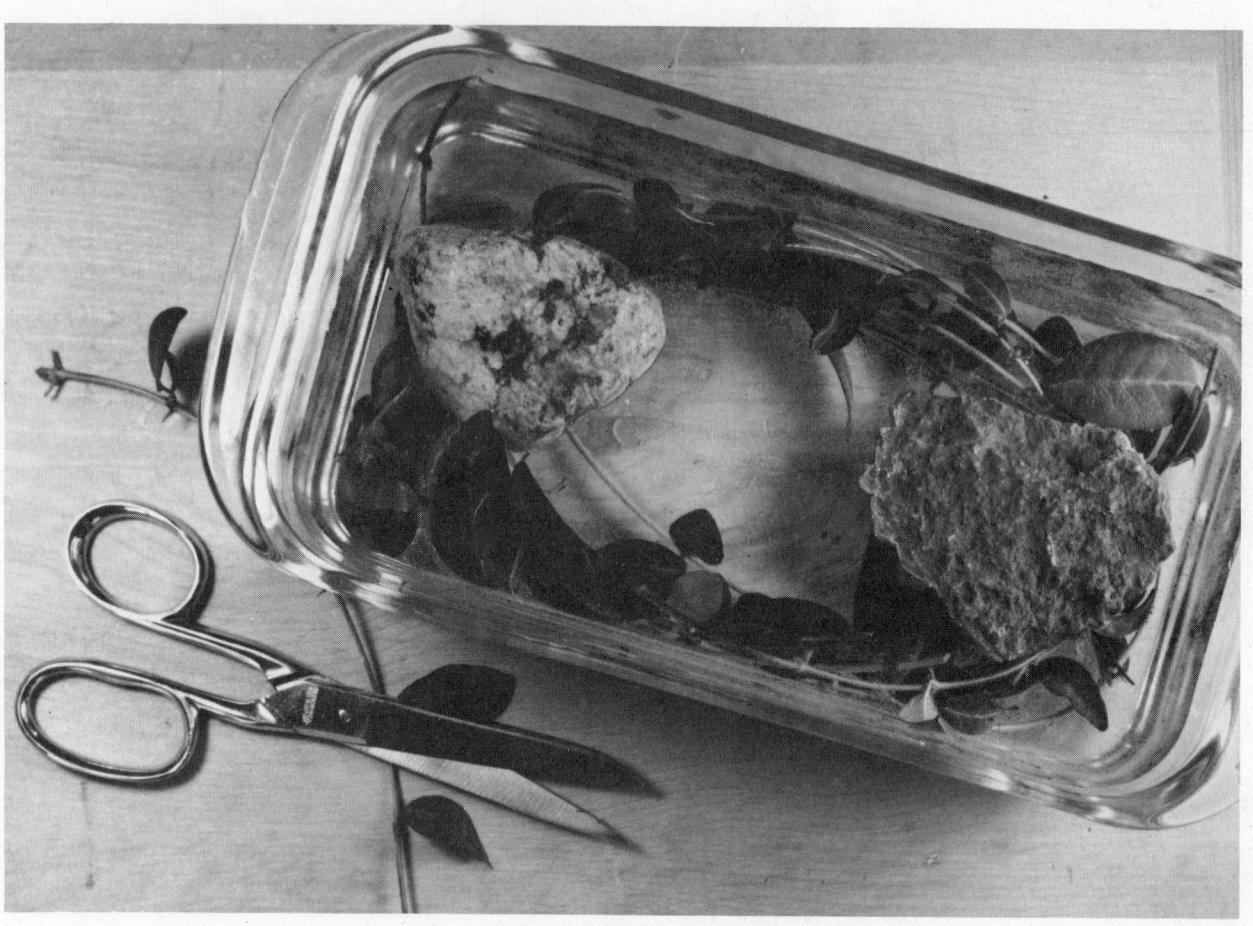
Processing periwinkle (myrtle) in glycerin. Small rocks help to keep the vines submerged in the solution.

It will not be too difficult to tell when the processing has been completed since most leaves, as they absorb glycerin, undergo a change in color. Some leaves will merely darken; others will turn various shades of tan, bronze, or mahogany. Barberry leaves, if gathered early in the season, turn a brilliant red.

STORING DRIED MATERIAL
Once dried, plant material need not be used immediately; it can be stored away and made up into arrangements at a later

Flowers processed in silica gel should be stored in tightly sealed containers.

time. Most dried plants will remain in good condition for many months, or even years, if they are properly protected from dampness and dust.

Dampness can ruin dried plant material very quickly. Not only does it promote the growth of unsightly molds, but it may also cause dried flowers to fade, shrivel, or wilt. Dust, while not as destructive as dampness, is often troublesome to remove, especially when it has accumulated over a period of months.

Flowers processed in silica gel are the ones most likely to be affected by dampness; they should, therefore, be kept in tightly sealed containers. Single blooms are best stored in large, wide-mouthed jars or coffee cans. Long spikes and

DRYING PLANT MATERIAL

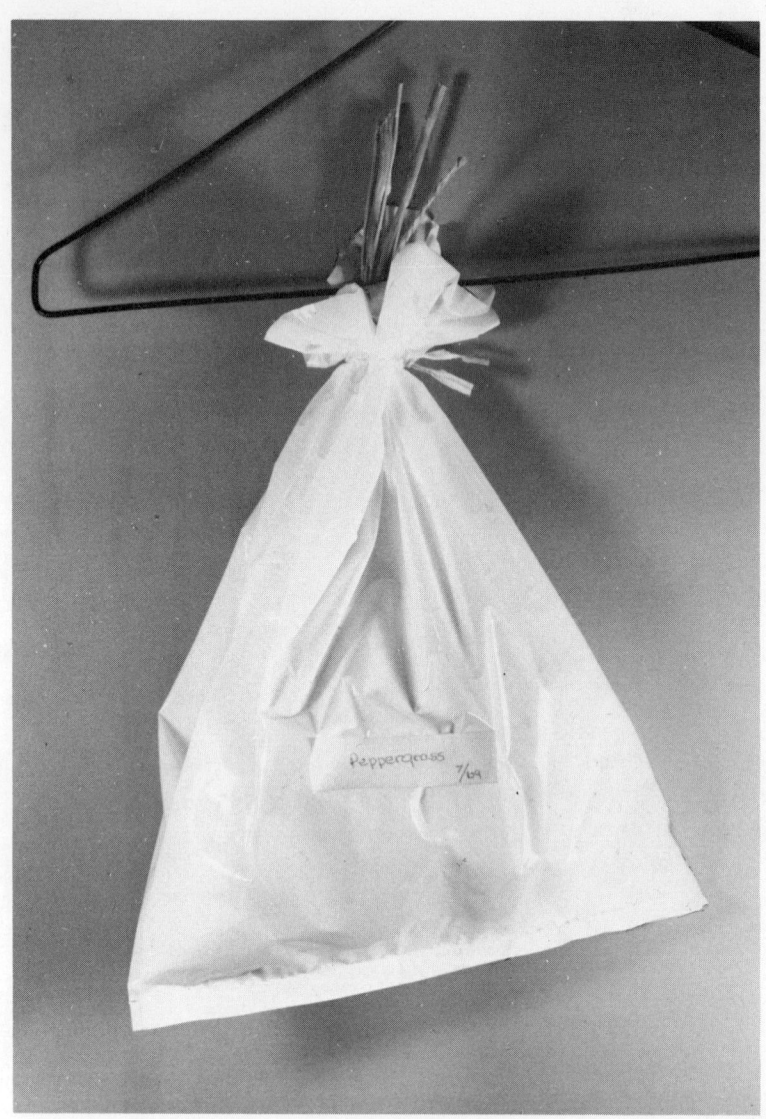

A bunch of dried material covered with a plastic bag to protect it from dust and humidity.

sprays of flowers are more easily stored in boxes. Sturdy suit boxes are ideal for this purpose.

Sprinkle a small amount of silica gel (one or two tablespoons) in the bottom of the container. Cover the silica gel with a thin layer of paper toweling and place the dried material on top. Avoid packing flowers too closely together. With masking or freezer tape, seal the cover tightly on the container and then store the container in a dry place. Glass containers should be stored away from the light to keep their contents from fading. It is a good idea to label boxes and cans so that later, when you wish to make an arrangement, the material can be easily located.

Air-dried material can also be stored in boxes, but when storage space is limited, plants can be covered and left hanging where they are dried. Plastic garbage bags make excellent dust- and moisture-proof covers. Put several tablespoons of silica gel in the bottom of a bag; slip the bag up over the bunch of dried material and secure it tightly around the plant stems with string or tape.

Foliage processed in glycerin is not affected by moisture and does not need special storage. However, after processing, leaves and branches that have been in contact with the glycerin solution may be sticky; these should be washed, and dried with a soft cloth. Then stand foliage in a clean can or jar. If you wish, foliage may be stored in boxes, but *do not add silica gel.*

2 GATHERING PLANT MATERIAL

Gather your plant material on a dry, sunny day. Plants gathered when the weather is damp or excessively humid take longer to dry and are more likely to mold in the process. Late morning and early afternoon are the best times for collecting material. Never pick plants when they are wet with dew. After a heavy rain, wait at least a day, so that the plants will have time to dry completely.

Use large, sharp scissors or shears for cutting plant stems. Even the most delicate flowers can sometimes have tough stems, and if you attempt to break them with your fingers, you may damage or destroy the remainder of the plant. A sharp penknife is often better than scissors for cutting woody stems or branches of foliage. Cut as long a stem as possible, particularly when the material is to be air dried.

Select your plant material with care. Use only material that is fresh and in good condition. In warm weather most plants wilt rapidly and should be processed as soon as they are gathered. Before drying flowers, examine them carefully and discard any faded or imperfect blooms. Also discard any material that is badly infested with insects. Remove all but very tiny leaves from the stalks of flowers, seedpods, and berries.

If thistle leaves are too prickly to handle, remove the leaves after drying by scraping the plant stalks with a knife.

Start collecting your material for drying as early in the season as possible. In this way you will be able to get a greater variety of flowers and other material for your arrangements. Plan a drying schedule. Spread the processing over the entire summer, gathering and drying some material each week. Check the flowering season of the various plants you want to dry, so that you will have some idea of when they must be gathered. A seed catalog, garden encyclopedia, or wildflower guide will give you this information.

It is a good idea to keep notes on the material you dry each year. Use file cards or a small notebook for this purpose. Write down the plant name, where and when it was gathered, and the method used in drying it. At the next drying season you will find these notes an enormous help in locating material and in recalling the most suitable drying method.

SELECTING PLANT MATERIAL FOR DRYING

Most flowers can be dried; but because they differ widely in structure, texture, and moisture content, some will dry better than others. However, as might be expected, no dried flower will look exactly as it did when it was fresh. All flowers shrink in drying because they lose their natural moisture. After processing, many are much smaller; with others, the shrinkage is barely noticeable. Very moist, juicy material may shrivel and lose its former shape entirely.

The flower color may also change in the drying process. It may fade, darken, and in a few cases disappear completely. Yellow, pink, and orange are the most stable flower colors. Blue is the most transient. Of the common garden flowers, only delphinium and larkspur retain their original blue for any period of time. The blue in some flowers lasts for a while, but eventually it turns grey. Lavender, is a more enduring color. The lighter shades of red sometimes deepen, while dark red and dark purple may dry almost black. In most white flowers that have been dried, the color turns creamy.

Changes in texture are more apparent in flowers with very thin or silky petals. Dried tulips, for example, are almost transparent when dried. Apple, cherry, and peach blossoms also change noticeably in texture. Flowers with thicker petals, such as zinnias, marigolds, and roses, have much the same texture

Large, ruffled marigolds and crab apple leaves are combined with the seedpods of moth mullein, poppy, and rough-fruited cinquefoil in a brass container.

as they had when fresh. As a rule most fragile-textured flowers shatter easily, and though they may dry satisfactorily, they rarely last long in an arrangement.

Garden Flowers

Many garden flowers make excellent subjects for drying. It would be impossible in a book of this size to mention all of them, but the species included in the following list are fairly common. Most of these flowers grow easily in average soil, and will hold their original color and shape quite well when dried. The best drying method to use is indicated by the letter following the plant name (if no letter is shown, another drying method is suggested in the text):

H—Air dry by hanging.
S—Dry with silica gel.
G—Process in glycerin.

Achillea—H. Two species of this perennial herb are particularly good for drying. *A. millefolium* (common yarrow) has dense, flat heads of yellow or rose-colored flowers. The Golden Plate variety is widely used in arrangements, and in the fall the dried flowers are sometimes available at florists. *A. ptarmica* bears small white blossoms. Flowers of the Pearl, a double variety, are occasionally tinted or dyed after drying.

Acroclinium (sunray)—H. One of the "everlastings," *Helipterum roseum* has rose-colored or white flowers with tapering, papery-textured petals. Gather them just as the buds begin to unfold. The flowers will open fully in drying.

Armeria (thrist)—H. The little rosy flower heads of *Statice armeria* are charming, especially for use in small arrangements. Do not confuse this plant with limonium, the florist's statice.

Artemisia (wormwood)—H. The flowers of artemisia are mostly insignificant, but the silvery-white foliage of some species is good for accent in an arrangement. *A. albula* (Silver King) is the one most often dried.

Aster—S. There are numerous forms of asters, some wild and some cultivated. *Callistephus chinensis* (China aster), the popular garden annual, can be dried quite successfully. Flowers come in various shades of rose and lavender, and also in white. Use the smaller-flowered varieties; they are the easiest to process.

Bells of Ireland (shellflower)—H. Widely used in both fresh and dried arrangements, the long sprays of *Moluccella laevis* are excellent for establishing line. Odd rather than beautiful, each small white flower of this plant is surrounded by a green, bell-like cup; hence its name.

Celosia (cockscomb)—H or G. The crested, ruffled, or plumed flower heads of *C. argentea* are exceptionally

Courtesy of the Library,
New York Botanical Garden

Asters.

GETTING STARTED IN DRIED FLOWER CRAFT

long-lasting when dried. A few dwarf forms of celosia are now available. These bear smaller-sized blooms that are more in scale with the average arrangement. Flowers are usually golden in color, or some vivid shade of red. Celosia is the only flower that can be preserved with glycerin.

Coral bells—S. Dry the slender stalks of *Heuchera sanguinea* in a horizontal position, as you would delphinium.

Dahlia—S. Of the various forms of *D. pinnata*, the pompoms are the most suitable for drying. The flower heads are heavy, and should be wired. (See Figure 2.)

Delphinium (larkspur)—S. When dried, the annual *D. ajacis* known as larkspur, and the perennial delphinium, *D. elatum*, retain their blue color longer than any other flowers. Because larkspur has smaller and looser spikes than delphinium, it is easier to dry. Besides the blues, there are white-flowering forms of both species. Larkspur also bears flowers in many shades of pink and lavender.

Echinops (globe thistle)—H. Long-lasting and easily dried, the perfectly round steely-blue heads of *E. sphaerocephalus* are much in demand for arrangements. The globes of *E. ritro* and *E. humilis* are smaller in diameter, but they are also attractive. Gather echinops before the flowers open.

Globe amaranth—H. The small, trim, thimble-shaped blooms of *Gomphrena globosa* have long been a favorite for winter bouquets. Do not gather the red-violet flowers of this everlasting until they are mature and fully opened.

Gypsophila (baby's breath). Familiar both in gardens and as a florist's cut flower, the misty, white-flowered sprays of gypsophila make good subjects for drying. *G. paniculata*, with its often double rose-shaped blossoms, is probably the most popular of the several species. Cut the sprays before the flowers are fully opened and stand them in a jar or vase to dry.

Helipterum—H. The dainty golden flower heads of *H. humboldtianum* make it one of the most attractive of the everlastings. Gather the globular clusters while they are still in bud. When dried, their color will last indefinitely.

Hollyhocks. Courtesy of the Library, New York Botanical Garden

The white- or pink-flowered *H. manglesi* (rhodanthe) is quite pretty, too.

Hollyhock—S. Dry individual florets of *Althaea rosea* in various stages, from buds to flowers that are three quarters open. Pink and rose are the best colors for drying. Use the single varieties and wire them before processing, as shown in Figure 2.

Honesty (moonwort)—H. Two species of this plant are grown primarily for their large ornamental seedpods that are frequently used in dried arrangements. The flattened pods of the annual, *Lunaria annua,* are nearly round; those of the perennial, *L. rediviva,* are more oval, and pointed at both ends.

Immortelle—H. As its popular name implies, *Xeranthemum annuum* is an everlasting. The large multipetaled blooms are strawlike in texture and come in a variety of colors. It is best to pick immortelles while they are still in bud.

Marigold—S. The marigold will dry satisfactorily provided its long, deep calyx is tightly wired to prevent the petals from loosening. The large multipetaled *Tagetes erecta* (the African or Aztec marigold) should be removed from the silica gel as soon as the outer petals have dried and then suspended upside down to complete the processing. This will keep the tightly compacted center petals from becoming moldy. The smaller blooms of *T. patula* (the French marigold) and *T. sigmata* do not need the additional air drying. Cement the outer petals of the dried marigolds, as shown in Figure 4.

Peony—S. Dry the smaller varieties of *Paeonia officinalis* and *P. albiflora* as you would the African marigold. Single and white-flowered types do not dry well.

Poppy—H. Most flowers of the *Papaver* species shatter too quickly to make them worth drying. The bulbous seedpods, however, are excellent in arrangements. Gather the pods as soon as the flower petals have fallen, and before processing, spray them lightly with an insecticide such as Raid.

Rose—S. All roses dry well except single forms and those with white or dark-red flowers. Cut roses in various stages of development, from buds to blooms three quar-

GETTING STARTED IN DRIED FLOWER CRAFT

Zinnia (Red man).
Courtesy of the Library, New York Botanical Garden

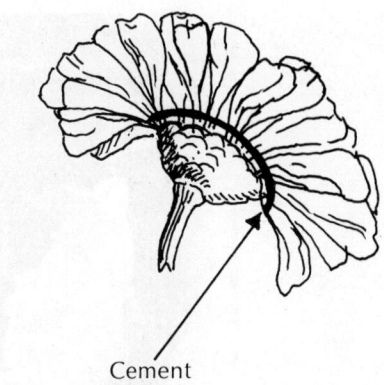

FIGURE 4 After drying zinnias, marigolds, and other multipetaled blooms, apply a heavy coat of household cement to the outer petals. Apply cement only at the base of the petals, as shown.

ters open. Small rosebuds can be air dried, if desired, and the foliage can be processed in glycerin.

Salvia (sage)—H. The blue-flowered *S. patens* and *S. azurea* hold their color fairly well, and are more attractive when dried than either the red- or purple-flowered species. Cut flower stalks before the buds are fully open.

Snapdragon—S. Use the small garden varieties of *Antirrhinum majus* in preference to the large, heavier-stalked hybrids. Dry snapdragons as you would delphinium.

GATHERING PLANT MATERIAL

Strawflower—H. *Helichrysm bracteatum* is perhaps the best known of the everlastings. Bunches of the dried flowers are frequently sold in florist and other shops. The flowers come in many colors, some with prominent yellow centers. Pick before the blooms are fully open, and dry in a cool spot. Wire the flower heads before processing. (See Figure 2.)

Verbena—S. The shapely clusters of *V. hortensis* come in many shades of pink, red, and lavender, and also in white. Flowers are frequently eyed or striped.

Zinnia—S. *Z. elegans* is one of the easiest of the garden flowers to grow, and with the exception of cactus-flowered varieties, dries extremely well. Glue the outer petals of zinnias after they are processed, as shown in Figure 4.

The tiny, strawlike flowers known as rockets are sold in many stores, and are useful for adding extra color to an arrangement.

GETTING STARTED IN DRIED FLOWER CRAFT

There are numerous other garden plants that dry well, but they require more exacting climate or soil conditions than the ones listed in the foregoing paragraphs. Some, such as heather, need an acid soil; others need a longer growing season in order to produce flowers.

Much of the pleasure of gardening and flower drying lies in experimenting. If you have a green thumb, try growing and drying some of the new or more exotic varieties of plants that you see listed in seed catalogs or offered for sale at local garden centers. The home garden doesn't have to be limited to flowers and foliage; it can provide a variety of other materials, such as popcorn, gourds, and ornamental grasses that will add interest to your dried arrangements.

Wild Plants

Fields, roadsides, woodlands, swamps, and coastal dunes offer a wealth of ready-grown material suitable for drying. At certain seasons, particularly in the fall, you will find wild grasses, seedpods, pine cones, and other material that is already dried and which needs only to be gathered and stored. Even in winter, oddly shaped roots, gnarled branches, driftwood, bracket fungi, and lichen can be found.

Because of differences in terrain, climate, and soil, the plant life of this country varies widely from one section to another. For instance, many wildflowers common to New England do not grow in the West; nor is one likely to find in the Rockies the plants that grow in the mountains of North Carolina.

The wildflowers and other plants included in the following list are common ones; you will undoubtedly find some of them growing in your area.

> **Alder** *(Alnus)*. Conelike fruit. Gather when dry and store in a box.
>
> **Barberry** *(Berberis)*. Foliage—**G;** berries—**H.**
>
> **Bayberry (wax myrtle)** *(Myrica)*. Foliage—**G;** berries—**H.**
>
> **Beebalm** *(Monarda)*. Seedheads—**H.**
>
> **Beech** *(Fagus grandifolia)*. Foliage—**G, H, or S,** depending on the desired effect. Also press. (See Chapter 4.)

GATHERING PLANT MATERIAL

Pods of butterfly weed, an orange milkweed.

Bittersweet *(Celastrus scandens)*—**H.** Remove red berries and use orange calyxes only.

Black-eyed Susan *(Rudbeckia hirta).* Flowers—**S.**

Burdock *(Arctium).* Flowers and spiny calyxes—**H.** Pick as flower begins to open.

Butter-and-eggs *(Linaria vulgaris).* Flowers—**S.** Dry as you would delphinium.

Butterfly weed *(Asclepias tuberosa).* Seedpods. (See milkweed.)

Buttonbush *(Cephalanthus occidentalis).* Ball-like fruit—**H.**

Cattail *(Typha latifolia)*—**H.** Pick early in the season. Spray with plastic spray.

Dock *(Rumex)* Seedheads—**H.** Pick at various stages for different color effects.

Evening primrose *(Oenothera biennis).* Seedpods—**H.**

GETTING STARTED IN DRIED FLOWER CRAFT

Closeup of dried field garlic. The tiny bulblets were removed from the base of the flowers after they were dried.

Closeup of dried dock.

Ferns (various species). Press. (See Chapter 4.)

Field garlic *(Allium vineale)*. Flowers—**S.** Carefully remove tiny bulblets after drying.

Field peppergrass *(Lepidium campestre)*. Seedheads—**H.**

Goldenrod *(Solidago)*. Flowers—**H.** Gather just as flowers begin to show color.

Hardhack *(Spiraea tomentosa)*. Flowers—**H.**

Hickory *(Carya)*. Buds. Gather in early spring and store in a box.

Joe-pye weed *(Eupatorium)*. Flowers—**H.** Pick before buds open.

Milkweed *(Asclepias)*. Pods. Gather and stand in a jar. As pods begin to split, carefully open them and scrape out the down and seeds. Finish drying.

Milkwort *(Polygala)*. Flowers—**H.**

GATHERING PLANT MATERIAL

Courtesy of the Library, New York Botanical Garden

Field peppergrass.

Goldenrod.

Hardhack, also known as steeplebush, is a small shrub that grows wild in open fields and pastures.

Moth mullein *(Verbascum blattaria).* Seedpods—**H.**

Mustard *(Brassica).* Seedheads—**H.**

Pearly everlasting *(Anaphalis margaritacea).* Flowers—**H.** Pick before flowers are fully open.

Pussytoes *(Antennaria).* Flowers—**H.** Pick early in the spring while they are still in tight bud.

Queen Anne's lace *(Daucus carota).* Seedheads—**H.** Gather as flowers fade but while seedheads are still green.

Rabbit-foot clover *(Trifolium arvense).* Flowers—**H.**

Rough-fruited cinquefoil *(Potentilla recta).* Seedpods—**H.**

Sea lavender *(Limonium nashii).* Flowers—**H.** Pick while they are still in bud.

Selfheal *(Prunella vulgaris).* Seedheads—**H.**

Sensitive fern *(Onoclea sensibilis).* Fertile fronds—**H.**

GETTING STARTED IN DRIED FLOWER CRAFT

Zinnias, field garlic, privet leaves, and the seedheads of Queen Anne's lace arranged in an ironstone pitcher.

Courtesy of the Library, New York Botanical Garden

Queen Anne's lace.

Closeup of dried sea lavender.

Smartweed *(Polygonum)*. Flower heads—**H.** Pick before flowers open. Spray with plastic spray.

Sumac *(Rhus)*. Berries. Pick when berries turn red, then spray with plastic spray and store. Stalks can also be stripped of berries and used in arrangements. (Do not touch the species with white berries, which is related to poison ivy.)

Sweetgum *(Liquidambar styraciflua)*. Fruit. Gather when it is dry and store in a box.

Tansy *(Tanacetum vulgare)*. Flowers—**H.**

GETTING STARTED IN DRIED FLOWER CRAFT

Closeup of dried thistles. The large flower on the left was trimmed close to the calyx before drying; the one on the lower right is untrimmed.

Stalks of staghorn sumac, with some or all of the red berries removed, are excellent for establishing the line of an arrangement.

Teasel *(Dipsacus sylvestris)*. Seedheads. Stand them in jar to dry.

Thistle *(Cirsium)*. Flowers (large species)—**H.** Gather unopened buds and flowers that are fully open. Trim purple part of flower even with calyx, and dry; or remove flower entirely and dry only the calyx.

Tulip tree *(Liriodendron tulipifera)*. Flowers—**S;** conelike fruit—**H.**

Vervain *(Verbena hastata)*. Flowers—**H.**

Virgin's bower *(Clematis virginiana)*. Feathery seedpods—**H.**

GATHERING PLANT MATERIAL

Delphinium and flower-of-an-hour (Hibiscus trionum) serve as the focal point of this pressed-flower picture.

Small but colorful strawflowers are mixed with graceful sprays of sea lavender and artemisia in a pale-green cream pitcher.

Winter cress *(Barbarea)*. Seedheads—**H.**

Yarrow *(Achillea millefolium)*. Flowers—**H.**

When you gather wild material, keep in mind that some native plants are now quite rare. Many states have passed strict laws which prohibit the picking of certain plants. Ground pine *(Lycopodium)*, dogwood, laurel, rhododendron, gentians, and trailing arbutus are some of the protected species. Also, never gather plants in a park, forest, or wildlife refuge belonging to the local, state, or national government.

Closeup of dried winter cress.

GATHERING PLANT MATERIAL

3
DRIED PLANT ARRANGEMENTS

When you have gathered and dried a nice variety of plant material, you are ready to start making an arrangement. This phase of your work with dried plants is perhaps the most enjoyable of all, for it provides a wonderful opportunity to be truly creative.

Making a dried-flower arrangement is in many respects no different from making an arrangement with fresh flowers. However, a distinct advantage of dried flowers is that they are not likely to wilt when for some reason you find that you cannot finish an arrangement immediately. As will be explained later in this chapter, there are also other advantages in using dried plant material.

TYPES OF ARRANGEMENTS

There are, in general, two types of flower arrangements, regardless of whether the material used in them is dried or fresh. The first type is the *line arrangement,* which is the more formal of the two. It is characterized by sweeping, well-defined lines that direct the eye toward a compact and well-defined focal point. The plant material in a line arrangement is

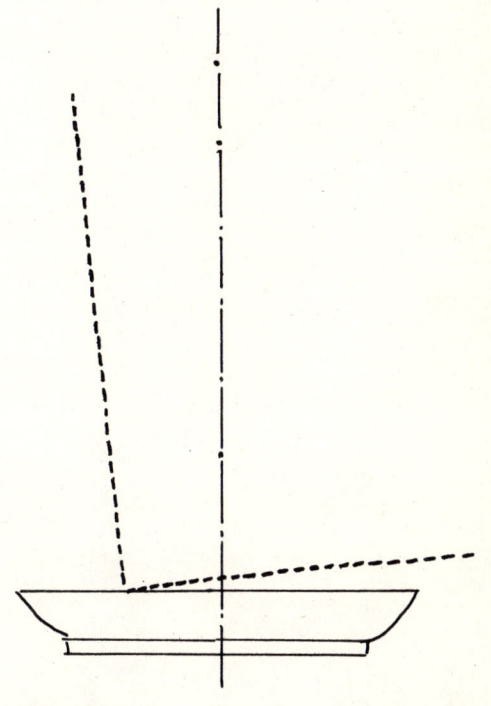

Basic design No. 1 for flower arrangements— L shape.

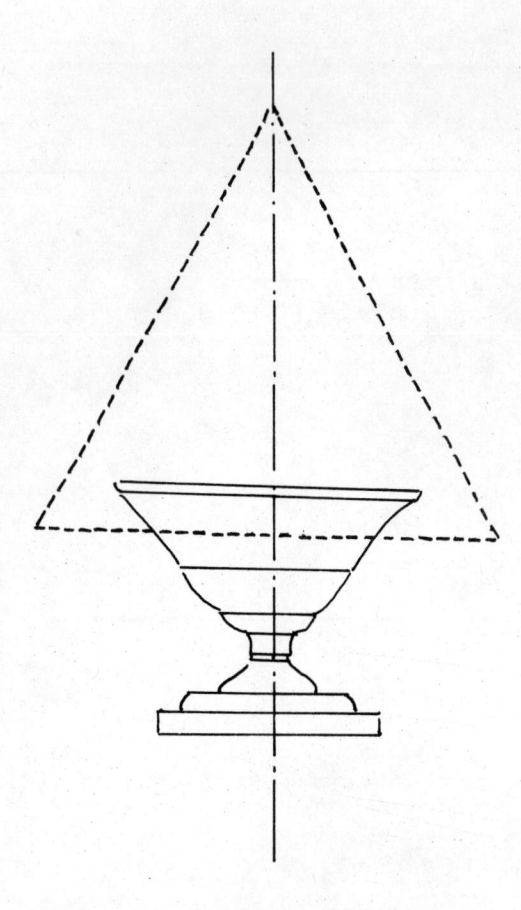

Basic design No. 2 for flower arrangements—Triangle.

usually distinctive in form and used with great economy. The second type is the *mass arrangement,* which is characterized by an abundant but well-organized use of material. With the current trend toward less formal décor, the mass arrangement is becoming increasingly popular.

Before you begin an arrangement, decide where you will place it when it is completed. Will it be set flat against a wall, so that no one will see the back of it? Or will it stand in the center of a table, where it will be viewed from all sides? Knowing these things in advance will give you some idea of what size and shape to make your arrangement.

CONTAINERS AND HOLDERS

Keeping in mind where your dried arrangement is to be placed, select a container to hold it. Since dried plant material requires no water, your choice need not be limited to the more conventional bowls, vases, dishes, and jars. Driftwood often serves well for line arrangements, as do large seashells and chunks of lava. In short, the container you choose can be made of almost any material, with the possible exception of glass. Though an opaque, milk-glass container would be satisfactory, a transparent glass container is rarely appropriate, for it is extremely difficult to camouflage flower stalks and the necessary but unsightly mechanics of the arrangement. Filling the container with sugar or white sand is sometimes recommended to overcome this difficulty, but the results are seldom satisfactory.

A container that is simple in form and of some neutral color is generally the wisest choice; a brightly colored or elaborately decorated one is apt to detract from the arrangement itself. Pillow-shaped containers, which are widely used by professional flower arrangers, are particularly good. And size, of course, is a most important factor; for instance, if the arrangement is to be used as a centerpiece for the dining table, the container should not be so tall as to create a barrier between the diners and thus make conversation difficult.

You will also need a flower holder or some kind of material to help anchor flower stalks and stems in the container. Sand, kitty litter, and vermiculite are excellent for holding flowers in place when the container is more than three inches deep. Because these materials are fairly heavy, they also

GETTING STARTED IN DRIED FLOWER CRAFT

A mass arrangement of many small pink, blue, and white flowers.

Mass dried flower arrangement.

GETTING STARTED IN DRIED FLOWER CRAFT

Mass dried flower arrangement.

Line arrangement.

DRIED PLANT ARRANGEMENTS

35

The interesting shapes of pressed flowers and leaves can suggest all manner of conventional and geometric designs.

Asymmetrical dried flower arrangement.

DRIED PLANT ARRANGEMENTS

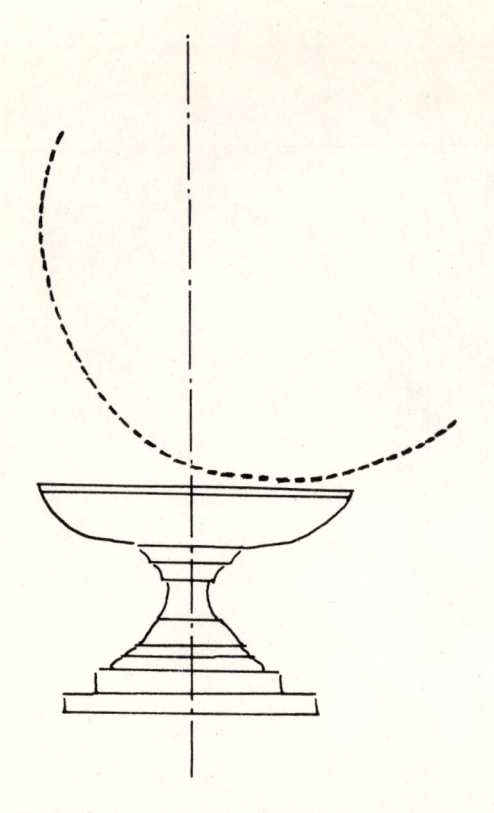

Basic design No. 3 for flower arrangements—Crescent.

Laurel leaves and various types of seedpods in an all-brown (monochromatic) arrangement.

serve as weights to prevent tall vases from being accidentally knocked over. Plasticine modeling clay makes a better flower holder for a shallow dish or bowl. Styrofoam can also be used for shallow containers, but unless the flower stems are wired, they are often difficult to insert in this material.

A pin holder is popular for use as a flower holder. If the pins are set too far apart to hold thin stems firmly in place, a little plasticine worked into holder will remedy the situation. A lump of plasticine will also keep the holder from sliding about in the bottom of the container.

GETTING STARTED IN DRIED FLOWER CRAFT

A saki cup serves as a container for a miniature arrangement of dried thistles, peppergrass, and crab apple leaves.

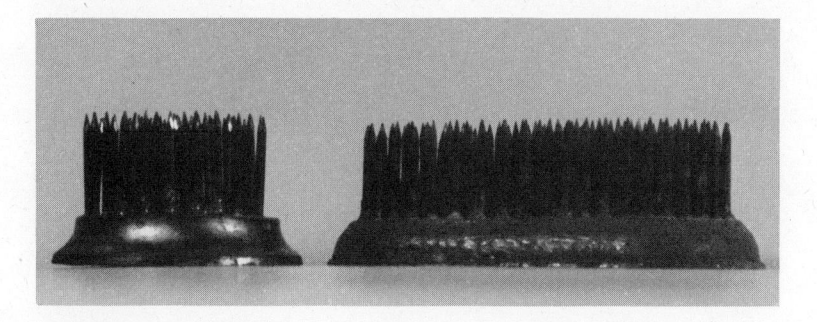

Pin holders.

DRIED PLANT ARRANGEMENTS

39

Mass dried flower arrangement.

GETTING STARTED IN DRIED FLOWER CRAFT

The silvery pompoms of dried thistles are combined with goldenrod and spikes of green-grey grass in a rice bowl container.

Triangular arrangement.

GETTING STARTED IN DRIED FLOWER CRAFT

When using one of the granular materials such as sand, fill the container to within approximately an inch of the rim. Gently force the stems well into the loose material, holding them close to their ends so that they will not bend or break off. When flower stems are very thin or brittle, pour out some of the granular material already in the container, and fill in the remaining space with a layer of plasticine.

Plasticine as it comes from the package is usually quite hard, and before it can be used it must be thoroughly kneaded until soft. When the clay is softened, press it into the bottom of the container, and carefully insert the flower stems. Using a finger, firmly tamp the plasticine around each stem to hold it in place.

Cut styrofoam slightly larger than the container and gently but firmly wedge it into place. Make small holes in the foam with an ice pick or nail; then insert the stems. If styrofoam and plasticine show in the finished arrangement, they can be camouflaged with small pebbles.

Besides a container and a material of some kind to secure the flower stems in place, you will, as mentioned previously, also need scissors, tape, wire, wire cutters, plastic spray, and cement. It is a good idea to have plenty of newspaper on hand as well, to spread both on top of your worktable to protect its surface and underneath the table to catch any bits of the dried material that may fall on the floor as you work.

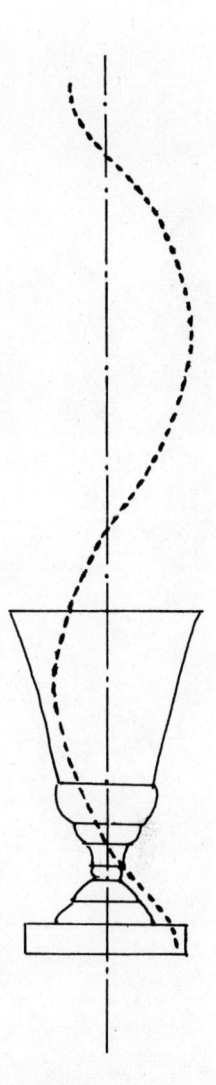

Basic design No. 4 for flower arrangements—S-curve (the Hogarth Curve).

SELECTING MATERIAL FOR AN ARRANGEMENT

Look over the various flowers, leaves, and seedpods that you have processed. At this point, if you have not already done so, you should decide whether the basic design of your arrangement will be a *line* or a *mass* composition. With the design and the intended location of the arrangement in mind, you can now select the appropriate plant material.

If the arrangement is to be a line composition, select material that is distinctive and somewhat bold in outline for the focal point. Also select some curved or oddly bent material with which to establish the composition line. Try not to use too many different types of plants. Remember that in a line arrangement the plant material should be used with great restraint.

DRIED PLANT ARRANGEMENTS

Bright vermillion rockets add an additional touch of color to a small arrangement of black-eyed Susans, rushes, poppy pods and sea lavender.

Line arrangement.

DRIED PLANT ARRANGEMENTS

Miniature arrangement in a Chinese teacup.

For a mass composition you will be able to use a greater variety of plants. If flowers are to be the focal point of the design, they should be somewhat larger or darker in color than the other flowers used. Select light-colored or finely dissected material for the margins of the arrangement. Plants such

GETTING STARTED IN DRIED FLOWER CRAFT

as dock and field peppergrass are excellent as fillers to give bulk to an arrangement.

As you select material, keep the size of your container in mind. If it is fairly large, choose fairly large flowers and leaves for the center of the arrangement. Small flowers and leaves would appear out of scale in such a container. In a small container very large flowers would make the arrangement look top-heavy.

Color is a very important factor in any design. In a flower arrangement there should always be one dominant color even when more than one color is used. The color scheme of your arrangement will depend on the colors of the various plants you have dried. If you have a good selection of dried material, you will be able to plan a color scheme that will harmonize or contrast with the surroundings in which your arrangement will be placed.

The material that you select for your center of interest should establish the dominant color. The main color can also be repeated elsewhere in the arrangement by material that is either the same color or various tints and shades of this color. A lesser amount of material of a second or third color may also be added. Dried plant material can be used quite successfully in monochromatic (one-color) arrangements.

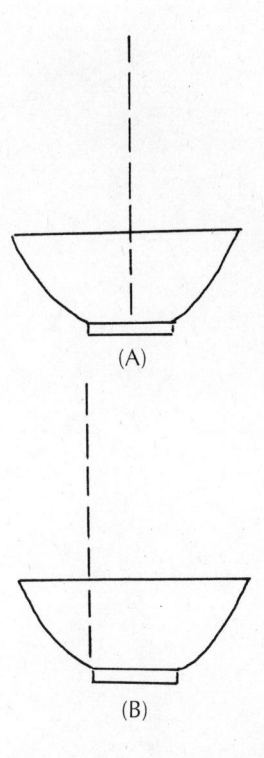

FIGURE 5 The line of a flower arrangement: A—symmetrical; B—asymmetrical.

MAKING A DRIED ARRANGEMENT

Begin your arrangement by placing the tallest material in the container first. If the arrangement is to stand against a wall, keep the tallest material well to the back of the container and arrange the other material in front of it. If the arrangement is to be viewed from all sides, place the tallest material in the center with the rest of the material around it. Use the very tallest stalk to establish both the height and the line of the composition. Make your arrangement about one-and-a-half times the height (or width) of the container. (Check the measurements with a ruler if necessary.) The line (vertical axis) of your arrangement may be either centered (symmetrical) or off-centered (asymmetrical). (See Figure 5.)

The material that is to serve as the center of interest, or focal point, is usually placed near the rim of the container, or in the case of a line arrangement, at a point where the lines converge. As you fill in your design, remember to place the

DRIED PLANT ARRANGEMENTS

heavier or darker-colored material at the bottom or center of the arrangement and the lighter material around the edges. Keep similar colors together to avoid a spotty appearance. You will find that small flowers are more effective when grouped together in bunches. If the line of the arrangement is symmetrical, balance your plant material so that both sides of the arrangement appear almost equal in weight. Turn the container as you work to insure that all parts of the arrangement that are to be visible are well filled in and attractive. When only three sides are to be seen, however, it is not necessary to fully complete the back. Cover up all wires and other mechanics so that they cannot be seen in the finished composition.

One advantage of working with dried plant material is that broken petals or fallen leaves can be repaired with cement, tape, or wire—an impossible thing to do with fresh plants. (See Figure 6.) Stems that are too short or those that have been cut to facilitate drying are easily lengthened with wire or provided with substitute stems (see Figure 7). Repaired or wired stems should be wrapped with floral tape (see Figure 8).

CARING FOR AN ARRANGEMENT

With reasonable care a dried arrangement should last for many months, or even years. As soon as an arrangement has been

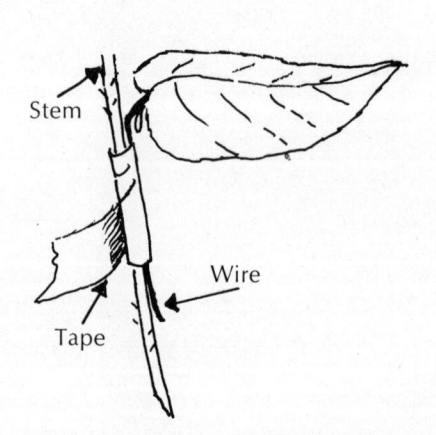

Small flowers can be grouped together and wired in bunches.

FIGURE 6 Fallen leaves can be repaired, or new ones added, with wire and masking tape. Use No. 18 or No. 22 wire for large leaves; No. 30 wire for small ones.

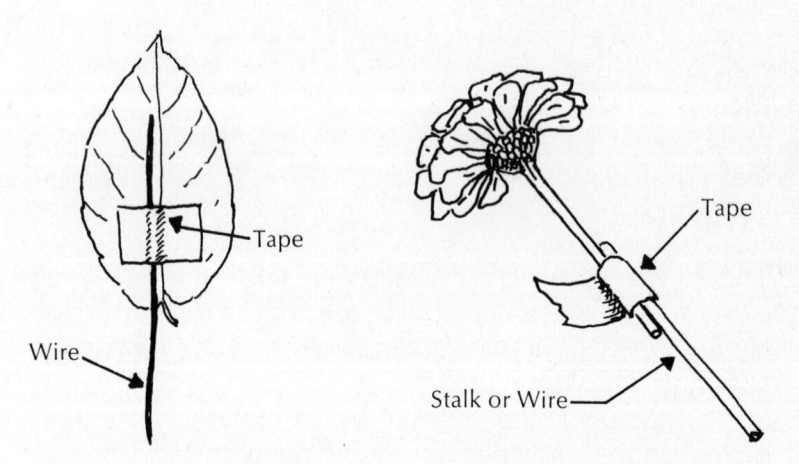

FIGURE 7 Lengthen or repair broken stems by taping a substitute stem or a piece of heavy wire to the short flower stem. Use masking tape for this, and then cover the joining with floral tape, as shown in Figure 8.

GETTING STARTED IN DRIED FLOWER CRAFT

An arrangement of zinnias, delphinium, wild yarrow, pink knotweed, grass spikes, and field garlic. When dried, the lavender garlic flowers loose their strong onion odor.

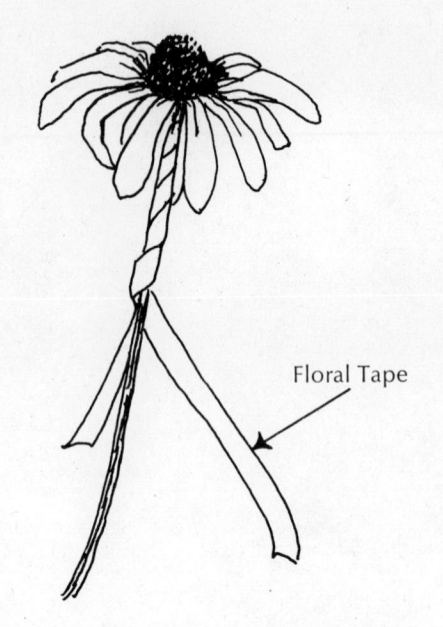

FIGURE 8 Wrap floral tape spirally around repaired or lengthened stems.

completed, it should be given three or four protective coats of clear plastic spray, such as Krylon. Hair spray—the regular type, not the supersoft—can also be used. Apply the spray according to the directions on the can, and allow ample time for one coat to dry before applying the next. The spray helps to strengthen the dried material and to keep the arrangement intact. It also makes it easier to remove any dust that may accumulate.

Go over an arrangement occasionally with a small camel's hair paintbrush. Wipe the dust off glycerinated foliage with a soft, damp cloth or a wad of cotton. Every few months freshen the arrangement with another coat of plastic spray. If some of the material loses its petals or begins to look dingy, remove it carefully and replace it with new material.

All dried plants fade in time, but the fading is usually so gradual that it will scarcely be noticed. Never place a dried arrangement in direct sunlight or too close to a radiator or hot-air register.

4
PRESSED-FLOWER PICTURES

Pressing is another method of preserving various types of plant material. Flowers and leaves dried in this manner will last for many years, and though seldom used in arrangements, they are excellent for making pictures and designs.

The growing popularity of pressed-flower pictures is understandable. The pictures are quaint, charming, and often quite beautiful. They are also easy to make—so easy, in fact, that many children as well as adults find flower pressing an absorbing hobby.

TOOLS AND SUPPLIES

The following lists all the materials that are needed for making a pressed-flower picture:

>   Plant material
>   Newspapers
>   Several old books
>   Rocks or bricks for weights

An arrangement of fire thorn, zinnias, and live–forevers.

Picture frame (with glass)
Illustration or matte board
Scissors
Small camel's hair brush
Household cement (Uncle Elmer's or Sobo)

Newspaper is used for absorbing the moisture squeezed from flowers and leaves as they are pressed. Heavy white blotting paper can be used for the same purpose and is often recommended, but newspaper is quite satisfactory and much less expensive. Use the regular black-and-white sections, for the colored or gravure-printed supplements are not as absorbent and when damp, their pages stick together.

Use one folded double-sheet of newspaper. Fold it in half, and then in half again. You will now have a sort of newspaper booklet with four quarter-sized sheets on either side of the center fold (see Figure 9). Fold the booklets in advance in order to save time when you are ready to do your pressing. You will need a good supply of paper, so here is your chance to get rid of those old newspapers that have been piling up in the basement.

If you prefer to use blotting paper for pressing, 8 inch x 10 inch sheets can be purchased from a commercial stationer. You will find it less expensive to buy blotting paper in bulk, one hundred sheets at a time. Unless a blotter is badly soiled after use, it can be dried out and reused several times.

The books will serve as your plant presses. (Use old ones that you do not care too much about, since the material that you are pressing between their pages may damage them.) Large, heavy volumes, such as old dictionaries and outdated encyclopedias, are particularly good if you happen to have them; but do not use books that have glossy, coated pages because, like the newspaper supplements, they are not absorbent enough to dry your material properly. A number of bricks or rocks placed on top of the books will add additional weight to your improvised press.

The width, contour, and color of the picture frame you select will be largely a matter of personal preference and taste. A plain, narrow frame usually looks best when the flowers and leaves in the picture are small and delicate. Very heavy or ornately carved moldings tend to distract the eye, and the picture—not the frame—should be the focal point. Attractive, ready-made frames are available in many shops; or you can

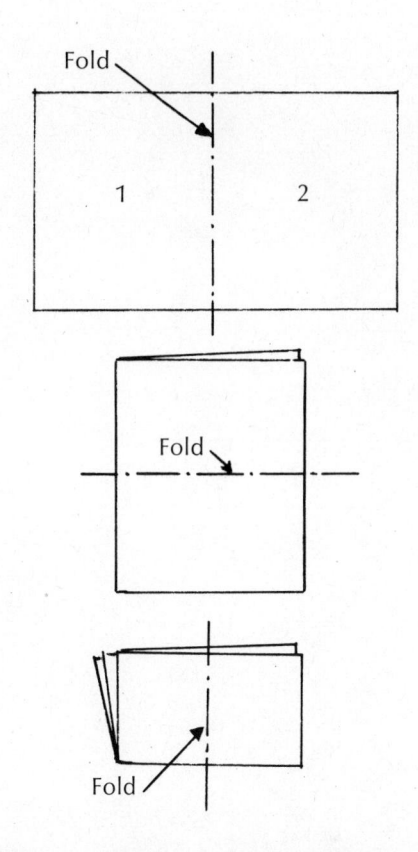

FIGURE 9 Folding a double sheet of newspaper to make a newspaper pressing booklet.

PRESSED-FLOWER PICTURES

FIGURE 10 The receptacle of a rose.

have one made to order. You might also use an old frame if you are lucky enough to have one stored away in the attic. You will not need a matte for your frame, since with pressed-flower pictures it is essential that the plant material come in direct contact with the glass.

A piece of matte board makes an excellent background for your arrangement and since it is fairly rigid, it is easier to handle than paper. Illustration board also works well as a background. If you would rather use paper, reinforce it from behind with a sheet of heavy cardboard. Illustration and matte boards come in various colors as well as in white and black, and they can be purchased wherever artists' materials are sold.

It is important that the background color provide sufficient contrast to the flowers, stems, and leaves that are to be placed on it. A white or cream-colored background is usually the best choice. With a black background, you may find it necessary to touch up thin stems with white poster paint, in order to keep them from being swallowed up in the dark.

SELECTING MATERIAL FOR PICTURES

The plant material used in pressed-flower pictures and designs is somewhat different from that used in dried arrangements. The flowers must be fairly simple in form. Complicated, multipetaled blooms such as marigolds and roses are difficult to press, and the end result is usually an amoebalike blob. Flowers with hard receptacles (see Figure 10) or large lumpy centers are also difficult to press, but their petals can sometimes be removed and used separately. Seedpods are rarely used. Most leaves can be pressed, though the leaves of herbaceous plants and vines are generally more satisfactory than those of the woody shrubs and trees. It is often hard to judge how a particular flower or leaf will press until you try it.

The color of a flower often changes in the pressing process. These color changes are not always predictable, and they can be quite surprising at times. For instance, a pink flower may change to purple, or a yellow one to orange. Many flowers turn brown, beige, or creamy yellow. Delphinium is the only blue flower that remains blue. Leaves also

Butterfly weed (orange milkweed).

change color; some turn brown; others, black; and still others stay almost as green as when they were picked. For some reason leaves and flowers pressed between newspapers seem to hold their colors better than those pressed between blotters.

It is important for the plant material to be dry when you gather it. The slightest trace of dampness or dew can cause furry spots of mold to develop on flower petals and leaves; or even worse, the material may be completely ruined. You will find that many flowers must be pressed immediately, or that a few, such as the white clover, are easier to handle if they are allowed to wilt a bit before you place them in your pressing book.

It is wise to leave a short stem on a flower or leaf whenever possible. Also gather extra stems and some larger stalks. These will serve to tie the various elements of your design

PRESSED-FLOWER PICTURES

together and create an illusion of motion. Without stems or stalks, a design will look stiff and bunchy. The best stalks are those that bend naturally or that can be made to bend into graceful arcs and curves. Trailing herbaceous plants and vines are ideal.

Leaves come in almost every shape and size imaginable, so deciding which ones you will use is mainly a matter of selecting the most attractive ones. Remember that leaves look better in a design if they are in scale with the flowers and other plant material. Do not hesitate to use a leaf "wrong-side-up" if it looks best that way. The undersides of some leaves are pale beige or silver grey, and provide attractive accents in compositions, particularly those with dark or black backgrounds.

The following flowers, leaves, and stalks are good subjects with which to begin your pressing activities. These represent only a few of the many plants that are excellent for pressing.

Flowers

* Anthemis
  Butter-and-eggs
  Buttercup *(Ranunculus acris)*
  Butterfly weed
  Clover, white
  Columbine *(Aquilegia canadensis)*
* Coral bells
* Cosmos
  Daisy *(Chrysanthemum leucanthemum)*
* Delphinium (larkspur)
  Goldenrod
  Hop clover *(Trifolium)*
* Hydrangea, white
  Jewelweed *(Impatiens capensis)*
  Marsh pink *(Sabatia stellaris)*
  Milkweed
  Queen Anne's lace
  Rough-fruited cinquefoil
  Sweet clover *(Melilotus)*
* Viola (pansy, violet)
  Wood sorrel *(Oxalis)*

---

* Garden varieties

GETTING STARTED IN DRIED FLOWER CRAFT

Leaves

    Barberry
    Bindweed *(Convolvulus)*
    Bramble (raspberry, blackberry, etc.) *(Rubus)*
    Burdock (Use the leaves from tiny seedling plants.)
    Cinquefoil
    Clover
    Coral bells
    Delphinium
    Echinops
    Ferns (various species)
    Herb Robert *(Geranium robertianum)*
    Ivy, English *(Hedera helix)*
    Japanese maple *(Acer palmatum)*
    Rose
    Vetch *(Vicia americana)*
    Virginia creeper *(Parthenocissus quinquefolia)*
    Wood sorrel

Blossoms of the rough-fruited cinquefoil.

Stalks

Bedstraw *(Galium triflorum)*
Bindweed (Use young end growth of vines.)
Clover
Vetch
Virginia creeper (Use young end growth of vines.)

PRESSING PLANT MATERIAL

You will need a certain amount of patience when pressing plant material. Prior to the actual pressing the plants must be

The bronze-green leaves of Virginia creeper used with Queen Anne's lace and creamy-yellow cinquefoil blossoms in a long panel design.

Virginia creeper.

GETTING STARTED IN DRIED FLOWER CRAFT

Pressed leaves. Top row (l. to r.): rough-fruited cinquefoil, hedge bindweed, burdock, bramble (underside of leaf); middle row: rose, common vetch, staghorn sumac; bottom row: ragweed, wood sorrel, privet, Virginia creeper.

carefully arranged in the pressing books. Arranging the material can sometimes be rather tedious, but to achieve good results—work slowly. Do not try to rush this part of the job. Remember—once a pressing book is closed, the plants will dry exactly as you have arranged them.

Do not gather too many things at one time. If the weather is warm, stand the material you have picked in a jar of water. This will keep it from wilting while you work. The wet por-

PRESSED-FLOWER PICTURES

tion of a plant stem should always be removed before the plant is placed in the pressing book.

Begin by inserting a newspaper booklet into one of your pressing books. Open the booklet along its center fold. If you intend pressing very juicy material, such as delphinium, place two or three booklets on top of the first one. Arrange your plants on only one page of the open booklet. Do not use the facing page. Space the plants far enough apart so that they do not overlap or touch one another, and place the heaviest material close to the center of the book. When you have completely filled the page, fold the facing page of the newspaper over it and gently close the pressing book. Insert additional newspaper booklets containing plant material into the pressing book at twenty-five-page intervals.

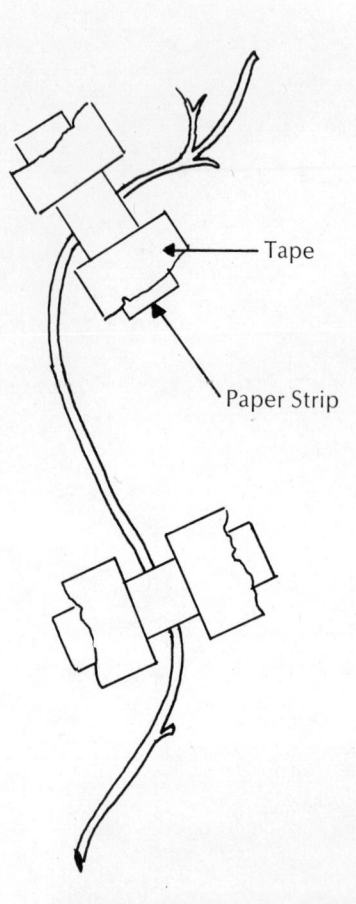

FIGURE 11 Stalks can be made to curve, before pressing, with paper strips and bits of masking tape. Do not tape directly on the stalk.

Rose petals and clover ready for use in a pressed-flower design.

GETTING STARTED IN DRIED FLOWER CRAFT

When you arrange your plants for pressing, make sure that all the flower petals are smooth and that the tips and edges of the leaves lie flat. You will find that most leaves are easier to flatten when they are placed face down on the newspaper; the same is also true of some flowers. Leave a short stem on a flower or leaf whenever possible. If, however, flowers or leaves cannot be flattened properly with their stems attached, snip off the stems and press them separately. They can always be reassembled later if needed, with the joinings discreetly hidden beneath other material in the design. Stalks that do not curve or bend naturally can be made to do so with paper strips and bits of masking tape (see Figure 11). Roll thick stems and stalks lightly with a pencil or rolling pin to flatten them before placing them in a pressing book. Press only the

Queen Anne's lace stored after pressing in a photographic blotter book.

PRESSED-FLOWER PICTURES

A pile of pressing books weighted down with rocks.

petals of roses and other hard-centered flowers, not the centers. When you make up the design, arrange some of the petals around a substitute center which has been removed from another flower.

GETTING STARTED IN DRIED FLOWER CRAFT

Before you close your pressing book, be sure to mark the page in some manner so that you will be able to locate the plant material when it is needed for a design. A long strip of paper extending beyond the pages of the book is a good means of identification; on it, write the date as well as the names of the various plants you have arranged on the page.

After each pressing session, pile your pressing books one on top of another, and weight the stack with several heavy rocks or bricks. Most plant material needs to remain in a pressing book for at least six weeks before it is dry enough for use. Heavy material may take longer. Once the material has been arranged in the books, it should not be disturbed until the six-week pressing period has ended. No matter how anxious you are to get started on a design, don't give in to the temptation to open the books any sooner; if you do, you may tear, wrinkle, or totally disarrange the plants.

ASSEMBLING A PRESSED-FLOWER PICTURE

Before you start assembling a pressed-flower picture, the illustration or matte board that is to serve as a background should be cut to fit the picture frame you have selected. Also, the glass for the frame should be thoroughly washed, then dried with a soft, lintless cloth or paper towel.

Choose a place to work where your flowers and other pressed material will not be upset by passersby, sudden drafts from windows and doors, or the wagging tail of the family dog. Then look over the plant material you have pressed and decide which of the flowers and leaves you will use in your design. Select large or colorful flowers as the focal point, and use long, gracefully curved stalks to give it a feeling of motion.

You can work up your design as you go along by moving the material about on the background. (Be sure your hands are clean before you begin.) To shift flowers and leaves from one part of the design to another, use a camel's hair paintbrush, which is better for this purpose than tweezers. Or if you prefer, first sketch out a design on a separate piece of paper. Never mark or draw on the background board, for pencil marks can sometimes be extremely hard to remove.

Don't use too much material in one design, or crowd it in such a way that the shapes of the flowers and leaves are lost in the confusion. Open areas can be as important to a

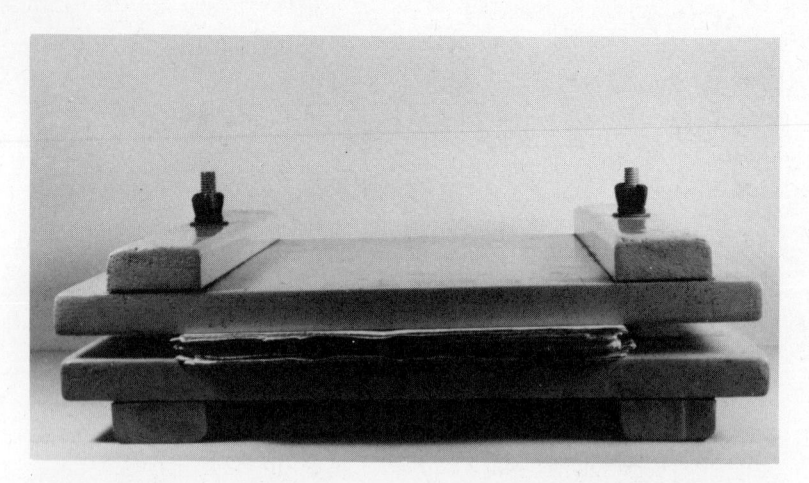

A plant press is sometimes useful for flattening lumpy-centered flowers before putting them into the pressing book. The press shown in the picture was homemade from scrap pine shelving.

A small camel's hair brush is useful for arranging pressed flowers and leaves on the background board.

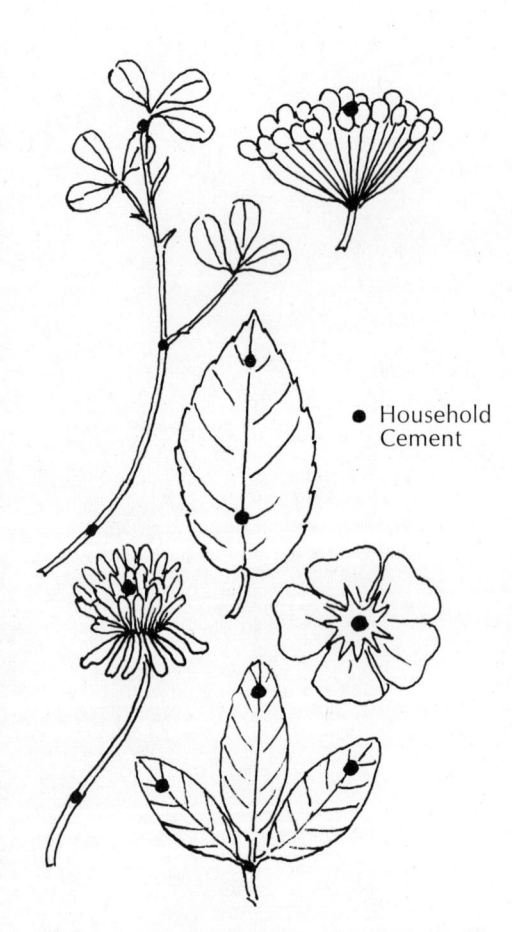

FIGURE 12 Apply tiny dots of cement to the undersides of flowers, leaves, and stalks.

good design as the flowers themselves. Try not to overlap the plant material or pile one thing on top of another.

When the flowers, leaves, and stalks are arranged to your satisfaction, anchor them in place with household cement so that they won't slide about when the design is framed. Squeeze a small amount of the cement onto a square piece of waxed paper; then, using the pointed end of your paintbrush handle, apply tiny dots of cement to the undersides of the

GETTING STARTED IN DRIED FLOWER CRAFT

Detail of a pressed-flower composition.

leaves and flowers. (See Figure 12.) Use the cement sparingly; otherwise, it may seep out from under the edges of the plants and stain the background. Just make certain that all the plants are fastened to the background and that there are no loose pieces.

After the design is completed, wait an hour or so for the cement to dry thoroughly; then cover the design with the glass of the picture frame. Holding the glass and the back-

PRESSED-FLOWER PICTURES

ground board with the design firmly together, slip them into the frame. Behind these, put hardboard or heavy cardboard to fill the back of the frame and to keep the design in contact with the glass. Now, with a pair of pliers, insert small brads or triangular glaziers' points along the edges of the frame to hold the glass, design, and backing board securely in place. As a finishing touch, you can, if you wish, cement a sheet of brown wrapping paper over the back of the frame to cover up the mechanics.

Your pressed-flower picture is now ready to display for your own pleasure and for that of your family and friends.

BIBLIOGRAPHY

Bolton, Eleanor R., *Dried Flowers with a Fresh Look*. New York, Van Nostrand Reinhold Company, 1958.

Booke, Ruth V., *Pressed Flower Pictures and Citrus Skin Decorations*. New York, Van Nostrand Reinhold Company, 1962.

Brownlow, Leroy, *Flowers That Never Fade*. Fort Worth, Tex., Brownlow Publishing Co., n.d.

Carico, Nita C., and Jane C. Guynn, *Dried-Flower Book*. New York, Doubleday & Company, 1962.

Clements, Edith S., *Flowers of Mountain and Plain*, 2d ed. Darien, Conn., Hafner Publishing Co., 1955.

Foster, Laura L., *Keeping the Plants You Dig*. New York, Thomas Y. Crowell Company, 1970.

McDowell, Pamela, *Pressed Flower Pictures*. New York, Charles Scribner's Sons, 1970.

Peterson, Roger T., and Margaret M. McKenny, *A Field Guide to Wildflowers of Northeastern and North-Central America*. Boston, Mass., Houghton Mifflin Company, 1968.

Petrides, George A., *A Field Guide to Trees and Shrubs.* Boston, Mass., Houghton Mifflin Company, 1958.

Seymour, Edward L., ed., *The Wise Garden Encyclopedia.* New York, Grosset & Dunlap, Inc., 1970.

Squires, Mabel, *The Art of Drying Plants and Flowers.* New York, Barrows & Company, 1958.

———, *Handbook of Dried Arrangements and Decorations.* New York, Barrows & Company, 1964.

———, *New Trends in Dried Arrangements and Decorations.* New York, Barrows & Company, 1967.

INDEX

Achillea. *See* Yarrow.
Acroclinium, 16
Air drying, 3, 16
Alder, 21
Anthemis, 56
Apple blossoms, 14
Armeria, 16
Arrangements, types of, 31, 32, 43, 46, 47
Artemisia, 16
Aster, 16
Baby's breath. *See* Gypsophila.
Background boards, 53, 54, 63, 65, 66
Barberry, 6, 8, 21, 57
Bayberry, 6, 21
Bedstraw, 58
Beebalm, 21
Beech, 21
Bells of Ireland, 16
Bindweed, 57, 58
Bittersweet, 22
Blackberry. *See* Bramble.
Black-eyed Susan, 22
Blotting paper, 53, 55
Books, pressing, 51, 53, 55, 59, 60, 61, 63
Brads, 66
Bramble, 57
Brush, camel's hair, 2, 4, 50, 53, 63, 64
Burdock, 22, 57
Butter-and-eggs, 22, 56
Buttercup, 56
Butterfly weed, 22, 56
Buttonbush, 22
Carnation, 5
Cattail, 22
Celosia, 6, 16–17
Cement, household, 2, 43, 48, 53, 64, 65, 66

Cherry blossoms, 14
Cinquefoil, rough-fruited, 24, 56, 57
Clover, hop, 56
Clover, rabbit-foot, 24
Clover, white, 55, 56, 57, 58
Cockscomb. *See* Celosia.
Color, 14, 47, 48, 54, 55
Columbine, 56
Containers, 32, 38, 43, 47
Coral bells, 17, 56, 57
Cosmos, 56
Dahlia, 17
Daisy, 5, 56
Delphinium, 5, 14, 17, 54, 56, 57, 60
Dock, 22, 47
Dogwood, 29
Driftwood, 21, 32
Drying methods, 2, 3, 15–16, 51, 58–63
Echinops, 17, 57
Everlastings, 16, 17, 18, 20, 24
Ferns, 23, 24, 57
Flower Dri. *See* Silica gel.
Foliage, 6–8, 11, 13, 19, 56, 57, 61
Garden flowers, 14, 15–21, 56
Garlic, field, 23
Gathering plants, 13–14, 29, 55–56, 59
Gentians, 29
Glaziers' points, 66
Globe amaranth, 17
Globe thistle. *See* Echinops.
Glue. *See* Cement.
Glycerin, 2, 6–8, 11, 16, 17, 19
Goldenrod, 3, 23, 56
Gourds, 21
Grasses, 3, 21
Ground pine, 29

Gypsophila, 17
Hardhack, 23
Heather, 21
Helipterum, 17–18
Herb Robert, 57
Hickory, 23
Holders, flower, 32, 38, 43
Hollyhock, 18
Honesty, 18
Hydrangea, white, 56
Immortelle, 18
Ivy, 6, 7, 57
Japanese maple, 57
Jewelweed, 56
Joe-pye weed, 23
Larkspur. See Delphinium.
Laurel, 6, 29
Leaves. See Foliage.
Limonium. See Statice.
Marigold, 5, 14, 18, 54
Marsh pink, 56
Milkweed, 23, 56
Milkwort, 23
Moonwort. See Honesty.
Mullein, moth, 24
Mustard, 24
Myrtle. See Periwinkle.
Newspaper, 43, 51, 53, 55, 60, 61
Pansy. See Viola.
Peach blossoms, 14
Pearly everlasting, 24
Peony, 18
Peppergrass, field, 23, 47
Periwinkle, 6, 7
Picture frames, 53, 54, 63, 65, 66
Plastic bags, 11
Plasticine, 38, 43
Plastic spray, 2, 22, 26, 43, 50
Pliers, 66
Popcorn, 21
Poppy, 18
Poster paint, 54
Pressing method, 3, 51, 58–63
Primrose, evening, 22
Privet, 6
Pussytoes, 24
Queen Anne's lace, 24, 56
Raspberry. See Bramble.
Rhodanthe. See Helipterum.
Rhododendron, 6, 29
Rolling pin, 61

Rose, 3, 5, 14, 18–19, 54, 57, 62
Sage. See Saliva.
Salvia, 19
Sand, 3, 32, 43
Scissors, 2, 13, 43, 53
Sea lavender, 24
Selfheal, 24
Sensitive fern. See Ferns.
Shellflower. See Bells of Ireland.
Silica gel, 2, 3–6, 9–11, 16
Smartweed, 26
Snapdragon, 5, 19
Statice, 16
Storage of dried plant material, 8–11
Strawflower, 20
Styrofoam, 38, 43
Sumac, 26
Sunray. See Acroclinium.
Sweet clover, 56
Sweetgum, 26
Tansy, 26
Tape, 2, 6, 10, 11, 43, 48, 51
Teasel, 27
Thistle, 14, 27
Thrift. See Armeria.
Tools and supplies, 1–2, 43, 51, 53
Trailing arbutus, 29
Tulip, 14
Tulip tree, 27
Vases. See Containers.
Verbena, 20
Vervain, 27
Vetch, 57, 58
Viburnum, 6
Viola, 56
Violet. See Viola.
Virginia creeper, 57, 58
Virgin's bower, 27
Waxed paper, 64
Wax myrtle. See Bayberry.
Weights, 51, 53, 63
Wildflowers, 21–24, 26–27, 29, 56
Winter cress, 29
Wire cutters, 2, 43
Wire, florist's, 2, 43, 48
Wood sorrel, 56, 57
Wormwood. See Artemisia.
Wrapping paper, 66
Yarrow, 3, 16, 29
Zinnia, 2, 5, 14, 20